also by april bernard

POETRY

Romanticism

Swan Electric

Psalms

Blackbird Bye Bye

NOVELS

Pirate Jenny

Miss Fuller

brawl
&
jag

poems

APRIL BERNARD

W. W. NORTON & COMPANY
Independent Publishers Since 1923
NEW YORK   LONDON

For information about permission to reproduce selections from this book,
write to Permissions, W. W. Norton & Company, Inc.,
500 Fifth Avenue, New York, NY 10110

For information about special discounts for bulk purchases, please contact
W. W. Norton Special Sales at specialsales@wwnorton.com or 800-233-4830

Manufacturing by Berryville Graphics
Book design by Chris Welch Design
Production manager: Lauren Abbate

Library of Congress Cataloging-in-Publication Data

Names: Bernard, April, author.
Title: Brawl & jag : poems / April Bernard.
Description: New York : W. W. Norton & Company, [2016]
Identifiers: LCCN 2015043967 | ISBN 9780393351736 (pbk.)
Classification: LCC PS3552.E7258 A6 2016 | DDC 811/.54—dc23 LC
record available at http://lccn.loc.gov/2015043967

W. W. Norton & Company, Inc.
500 Fifth Avenue, New York, N.Y. 10110
www.wwnorton.com

W. W. Norton & Company Ltd.
Castle House, 75/76 Wells Street, London W1T 3QT

1 2 3 4 5 6 7 8 9 0

brawl
&
jag

contents

I

II

I

Anger

1.

When in a farmhouse kitchen that smelled
of old rinds and wet cigarette butts
I hoisted the shotgun to my shoulder
and aimed but did not fire it at the man
who had just taken my virginity like a snack,
with my collusion, but still—

When I sat in a conference room
in an inquisition
at "the newspaper of record,"
across from the one slurping his pipe,
the one arching her eyebrow,
and I felt the heat like a wet brand in my chest,
repaid insult for insult and left their fancy job
like a squashed bug on the floor—

When I was twelve, too old, the last time
my father spanked me, pants down,
because I had "distressed" my mother
and my vision went red-black and
I did not forgive—

When, during my travels along the Gulf Coast,
the intruder returned in the night
and I did not call the cops again but stood
with a butcher knife facing the door, yelling, "Come in!"
although this time it was just the wind flapping
and banging the screen door—

When across a skating-rink-sized glistening table
I told the committee chair and her brooch I was a fan of Marx
and lost the fellowship—

When I threw a pot of hot coffee
and it just missed a man's head, and the black-brown spatter stains
were still there four years later long after he'd left me
and I finally moved out of that East Village hole—

2.

I would have had to be *thinking*
in order to have thought—loaded, not loaded?
—and I was not thinking, I was only dripping hot
and oh the pleasure, I can still feel its prickling,
crackle over the furnace of my rage,
to see his face go pale, his eyes widen,
his "put it down, put it down"—and I
put it down and allowed my life as well as his
to go on.

3.

I miss my anger. Decades go by
when all I can muster is absent-minded invective,
you know, directed at the news;
or a brief fantasy
of shoving someone
in front of a truck. Yesterday
I slammed my fist on my desk
and then apologized, to the desk.

Consider the tapestry
of the seven deadly sins, at Saint-Denis:
Anger, wild-haired and half-dressed,
picked out in blue and silver thread bunched
against the crimson,
rough against the fingertips, she
rides a black boar dappled with blood
and waves her double-headed axe—

Yes I remember her.
I always lie when I always say
I didn't know the gun was loaded.

Blood Argument

You insist
that the world belongs to a stony-hearted goat-god—
how every time we act, we enact
his vileness; how this is no
ecstasy, just a bad labored joke.

Your body in spasm
longs to strip the flesh, but if you do
there will be nothing left but the busy
bone-clatter of tactics.

.

I will listen instead to the river,
cold as time, smelling of blood-brown leaves.

Across the Lawn

A shriek of disgust:
>   the cat had sinned
>   against my mother
by pissing in her shoes.

He was afraid of our new biting puppy, as,

>   secretly,
was I.

The cat was mine; he had delivered me
from adolescent insomnia
>   by sleeping in my bed.

>   Every afternoon he purred and dozed
>   on my lap;
I fingered his broad black-padded paws
each with two extra toes, and he
>   put his claws out,
pulled them in,
>   as I read myself into the dusk.

A sudden shout from my sister,

>   pointing
out the window—I looked
to see, across the lawn:

                    Pale figures
against the dark of the trees:
My father walking with a bunched-up towel,
my mother following with a spade.

                                    It took
so long for me to understand—

I know   now
                        they used chloroform
and buried him in the woods then refused
to talk about it and sent my sister to her room

as I said nothing
                        and did not cry out,
                                        did not
say one word—

Still today I can see them,
                        as if from a great distance,
pale, in grim progress across the lawn.

Again I delay knowing
                        what they are doing.

Paean for the Players

The pale actor's mouth
opens oddly, an envelope
filled with ink, no teeth.
The effect seems apt
for the tormented Prince
who gouts words
onto the thick cream
paper of the air; we
see down the well
of words a terrible pink
tongue, the mortal man
in pieces predicting final
dismemberments.

Once briefly a player
myself I made the headlong
dash one must
against the words, against
death that would stay us.
When actors speak and move
we all become more
real, guising our best
versions of that
tenderness, ire, lust,
sad gaiety, as two fingers
pluck and ruffle and
unbutton a sleeve.

Bloody Mary

Note who's got to go
today, don't fuss
about the means,
just go ahead behead,
impale, starve, strappado,
the assortment
of choices enough
to make a crown
crow. They never
loved me enough.
It must be said: They
were a disappointment.

When divine mother
love wears out, I
reverse the robe
from blue to red.
I like a flat ground
to build the next town,
city, empire of disgust.
All the waste you see,
that's what I did,
none of that *happened*
to me. I did that.
I made that. I killed that. I.

Liliya in Omchak

1.

Late winter, and I
was such a little girl
when the wolves, the last
seen in those parts,
came into the town,
prowling, mad for food.
A long grey tongue
drooped over red gums
and frothy teeth shone
as one hugely nosed,
panting, into our garden:
It looked straight at me
through the window and I
was too scared to scream.
The men were gone on a hunt;
Aunt Magda got the rifle
and shot them, first
the one at our steps,
blew away its face;
then the other, running
and limping down the street
past the train tracks.
I could scream then.

2.

The blasted wolf-face
was wet and grey and white
and tangly spilling red.
The boys ran and kicked
its head like a ball, shouting.
We built a fire from scrap
wood and logs we stole
from Old Peter's pile.
We burned the wolves
and did not think until later
we had burned good meat.
Our mothers never even
tried to stop us.

3.

Even the lingonberries were gone
and we had eaten both
the ponies by the time
the men returned from the hunt
with nothing. So they drank.
The story of meaty wolves
wasted in their absence
filled them with rage.
My oldest brother, bigger
already than our father,
pushed Aunt Magda
down the cellar stairs
and broke her jaw. We hid
in corners the long weeks
until spring. Then the fish
ran again in the river
and the western railroad
returned with food in cans
and flour and salt and seeds
for planting. The men hitched
themselves to the plows and we
were needed in the fields to steer
and to hoe, very careful
for always until now, here,
about which stories to tell.

Carnival

They drove you around blindfolded
before dumping you in the suburbs.
Out on a lawn you sang
like a night-jar from the shadows.
Dawn nearly killed you
with its smoke, your lungs were on fire,
and those rude jokes from the passing cars—

Ambition can take you to the heights
or to the depths. The door chimes, useless,
a ding-dong pity. You labor to laugh,
to say your name—Go ahead, make something up—
It can't be as bad as all that—

Quickly, now: Over there is the carnival,
shining gold and red in the noon light,
                    hurry along and join it.

Thunder Mountain-Mesa-Valley-Ridge

The horse has lost its rider, and comes
into town at a shuffling half-gallop,
saddle sliding off into the dust.

This can mean only one thing: Apache.
Or the McLaren brothers. Fever.
Mountain lions. The Seven Nations. Zapatistas.

A tall pale man in tall boots—suitably laconic—
has been waiting fifty-five minutes for this,
his firing pin, to cock, and he mounts his horse.

Complication: The woman who always scolds
hits him with a broom so she must be restrained
and kissed before he departs.

Riding now, through desert scrub,
his tiny horse under a huge sky passes
mesas and chimney rocks, vista-vision of his epic as

behind the flat light lurks the menace,
the bear-man-lion-gang-tribe that mutters thunder music
from the mountains, then hushes, ominously.

Smoke signals. Tell-tale signs of snapped twigs.
Dead bodies by a campfire, ravaged by pox. Look:
Claw marks, a broken arrow tip.

Next the screen goes those queasy shades
of day-for-night, so it's like a night lit by too many
moons. Hoots of an owl that is not an owl.

Sudden violent chords and cymbals!
Gunshots! Men with open mouths!
A hurled hatchet thunked into a tree!

The tall man swings his body into fists,
wounded but unstoppable, all the way
to making his story right, all the way in fact to

a glorious show-down dance that pauses, lunges,
waltzes a bloody ten or so twirls, pauses, smashes.
The enemy always fights dirty, so he has to die.

The long pause, here, is for running children and wagons
crossing the town square, such as it is, as the false fronts
gape at ordinary life and ordinary order, until,

solemn as a church steeple, the tall man returns to business,
which involves whittling or whistling
or downing a whiskey and again waiting.

Beyond the town, the landscape, emptied of trouble-makers,
is allowed to sit still under cloud-wisps that hold no storm.
It is vast, and better now, with no one at all in it.

Else

At the first instance, to amuse others,
there was no stopping my wit—

It was like salt and pepper
all over the picnic—

Later, alone in the lamplight of my study,
my soul's true scent began to warm—

And now? Neither laughter nor tears,
but something else, better perhaps.

Found Sonnet: Samuel Johnson

(*from* Rambler, *No. 5*)

When a man cannot bear his own company
there is something wrong. He must fly
from himself, either because he feels a tediousness
in life from the equipoise of an empty mind,
which, having no tendency
to one motion more than another
but as it is impelled by some external power,
must always have recourse to foreign objects;
or he must be afraid of the intrusion of unpleasing ideas,
and, perhaps, is struggling to escape
from the remembrance of a loss, the fear of a calamity,
or some other thought of greater horror.

A French author has advanced this seeming paradox,
that *very few men know how to take a walk.*

Werner Herzog in the Amazon

his words to Les Blank in the documentary Burden of Dreams

We are challenging nature itself
and it hits back, it hits back, we have to accept
that it's much stronger than we are:
Fornication and asphyxiation
and choking and fighting for survival and growing and
just rotting away. The trees are in misery
and the birds are in misery. I don't think
they sing, they just screech in pain.

It's a land that God, if he exists, has created
in anger. Take a close look
at what's around us: overwhelming and collective murder.
And we, in comparison to the articulate vileness
of all this jungle,
we only sound like a badly pronounced
and half-finished sentence
out of a stupid suburban novel.

We have to become humble
in front of this overwhelming misery and
overwhelming fornication,
overwhelming growth and overwhelming
lack of order. Here
even the stars in the sky
look like a mess.

I say this all
full of admiration for the jungle.
It is not that I hate it—
I love it, but I love it
against my better judgment.

Lids

what was it you meant when you said
her hat is tragic

break it down for us, in the ready realm
of camp exaggeration

and the helmet in question, we both saw it
probably hand-made

with ear flaps that made the wearer
resemble a sort of bull-dog doge

and we remember with horror
what arrived hand-made by a grandmother

with a crochet hook and thick bristly yarn
oatmeal flecked with red

for Christmas and then tugged itching over my ears
every morning as my mother sent me off on the school bus

that was indeed tragic and could be diagrammed
with a rising action of skin rash and climax

of the hat left strategically
on the playground, long gone

but then in the denouement retrieved by my older sister
with triumph from the lost-and-found

and meanwhile you are right
more than half the hats I saw

on my last trip to the city
were certifiably tragic, officially tragic

drooping or perching or mannishly tugged
over hair being, also tragically, molded

although I did see one woman
in maybe the ugliest hat ever, dingy plum

with a studded leather band
who wore it with an air both tragic and heroic

as if walking to the scaffold, suffering
beneath the vagaries of whatever fashion she had misread

bear in mind that I own at least twenty hat boxes
nesting twice that many hats each pillowed in tissue

tricorne with emerald cock feathers
pale purple beaver felt fedora

black large-brim straw with black velvet band
a clutch of other straws one with faux cherries over the half-brim

at one time in my extreme youth
there were two milliners in the city who kept my hat size on file

let us not forget the silver beret, the black beret, the tweed beret
the circa 1912 dark brown beaver that sheds the rain

the white mink and cream cashmere pillbox
the beaded cloche

though tragedy was quick to arrive in those years
I promise you it was not on my head

and now I am thinking about epic
and how it would be good to have an epic hat

possibly of azure tulle netted about a crown of grey felt
and ready for rough seas

II

Wren

What I look for lives in looking.
A brown wren marked me in July:
Three days in a row, it circled the house at dusk,
paused to sing loud
a command—was it to go?—
and shook with the effort, tail
in a bob-dance high over its back.

Wordless seems a paradise to one
made of too many words.

Here I am:
Exiting the house, the theater, the memorial service,
exiting the classroom, exiting the restaurant—
gathering my things, smoothing my coat, exiting
into the warm and private night.

If the yellow moon

tonight is right, there may be a way to go on.
Through air so thick it wobbles a halo,
to a familiar face tipped up, she says:

"Though many have died, you are no
shadow. Notice: I am full and yellow.
You have little, nothing, not much,—but with me you abide."

September, and

the smell of late summer:
three rusty trawlers
coming late into port, slow past the lighthouse,

shuddering with the weight of the catch—
clumsy in the fog, barely able
to make their way by the dim stars.

City-Born

A vision, the first you see as a baby
grappling with the cutting away of the veil,
the letting in of the almost-hurt that is light—
Or the first words you hear as a halo of sound,
sheep or traffic baaing, an orchestral greeting.
Light and sound together creep in
to the cradle, around the corners of buildings,
and the city owns you. It is a perfect autumn,
despite the cross that awaits, that you cannot
yet see. In your first evening in this world,
pomegranate fills our mouths. It is a little tart;
let me taste it first for you.

Blossom

White, smudged like pastel on paper, like an orchard
May-blurred on the hillside
White like the light in the door as it opens

White as the robes of Tang mourners in the scroll
where the landscape slides into script,
vertical calendar of a dead man's life

White as the page these lines sit upon
puckering the rice paper with brush-strokes
that this side, the side that is life, has drawn

Gone into light he is now everywhere light is
I see and reach
but my hands are thick with shadow

He left in spring light
and threw stars from the shattered blossoms
on our sleeves and hair

It is not that I would drag him back—

I ask instead that the scent of light carry forward
this moment and the next
That the brush meet the paper not as blot but as sign

So what was formerly shadow may become a whiteness
White in the light of the door as it opens, blossom
of light perpetual in all places we yet go

Jacksonville, Vermont

The tree that went blurry
                    with blossoms
                                the week you died
is now stark black,
unleaved, its pears
frozen gold-brown drops—

Tonight I'm going to drive
and find that bar, the one we liked
                        in Jacksonville

and ask some man to go out back

so he can push me up against a truck,
taste beer-sweat like pear-juice,
sweet cunty death-in-life—

We'll meet as we are meant to

                        I'll cry out

for that   's the way

                        and all

in your honor

'Tis Late

Of course the tall stringy woman
draped in a crocheted string-shawl
selling single red carnations
coned in newsprint the ones
she got at the cemetery
and resells with a god bless you
for a dollar that same woman
who thirty years ago
was a graduate student
in playwriting who can and will
recite "At the round earth's
imagin'd corners, blow—"
announces silently amidst her louder
announcements that the experiment
some amateurs mixed of
white fizzing democracy
with smoky purple capitalism
has failed. We already knew that.
Her madness is my madness
and this is my flower in a cone
of waste paper I stole from
someone's more authentic grief
but I will not bless you
as I have no spirit of commerce
and no returning customers
and do not as so many must

actually beg for my bread. It is another
accident of the lab explosion
that while most died and others lost legs
some of us are only vaguely queasy
at least for now
and of course mad conveniently mad
necessarily mad because
"'tis late to ask" for pardon and
we were so carefully schooled
in false hope schooled
like the parrot who crooks her tongue
like a dirty finger
repeating what her flat bright eyes deny.

The Hyrtl Skulls

In a glass-front case taller than I, running thirty feet or so
along the upper gallery of a nasty museum of medicine in Philadelphia:

the skulls. One hundred and thirty-nine, collected
in the mid-19th century for Dr. Josef Hyrtl—"My pupils

who are physicians to the Turkish Pashas procured most of them
for me," he wrote—while others fanned out

to prisons and hospitals in Italy, North Africa, Greece, Albania,
collecting heads off the newly dead, measuring them,

noting geography, name, and cause of death if known.
Imagine all those bodies missing heads.

Here's one: Southern Carpathians. Gregor Spinik, age 15, Potter.
Died of Tuberculosis in the Charity Hospital, Vienna. Frontal bossing.

Here's another: Magyar Geysa Fehete de Galantha, Calvinist,
Hussar, deserter, guerrilla. Died in Munkacs, 1869.

•

Jesus met the woman at the well.
Jesus said, Where, where is your husband?

The woman said, I have no husband.
Jesus said, Woman, you have five husbands.

And the one you live with now
is not your own. The woman said, This man—

.

Some skulls are white, others a delicate mottled
golden brown. Most lack teeth. They look polished,

but that may be a trick of the light. Or maybe
the acid solution that burned off the flesh

of the suicide, the hanged man, the hapless drunk
and all the others was just caustic enough—

just caustic enough to singe the skull bones
to that comely golden brown, like the fake old vellum

of a fake old globe in a catalogue of fake things
you can buy. Here's another:

Slovak (Southern Carpathians) Olek Kubin, age 38,
Calvinist, Suicide by hanging.

And: Peter Lukacs, age 24. Gypsy.
This man, this man must be a prophet.

At the well: Jesus, woman, water, bucket,
husbands, five, not yours, not anyone's.

I have had five husbands, and the one I live with now
is not my own. This man must be a prophet.

Dr. Hyrtl was cataloguing race traits,
all the rage in the 1800s.

Almost by accident, the collection has come in handy
recently: Hyrtl skull DNA samples helped

the war crimes tribunal in The Hague say for certain
the mass graves at Srebrenica were full of Bosniaks.

.

Karbardine, Caucasus. Male. Moslem. Deformity due
to premature closure of the coronal suture.

Anonymous, male. For crimes of grave insubordination
died under the most cruel scourging. Russia.

I discover how primitive I am. If
I could, I would steal

all the skulls in Dr. Hyrtl's collection
and give each a burial. With the name,

if known, said aloud—a life in paraphrase. Also a hymn:
"Leaning on the everlasting arms"

would be good. Leaning and everlasting. Here,
here, where are your husbands?

Comet

I saw it one night
from the garden terrace,
swimming across the sky
like a fish in flames.
Once it was in my eyes
I could see nothing else,
I stumbled over the mountains
and valleys of my life
as one possessed,
as if these people and these days
had no meaning,
as if the fire in my eyes—
Della Robbia-blue,
eft-orange, and sulphur
—would keep me burning
with the immortals, as if
every last bit of me
had not already
gone to ash inside.

Not from the Italian

1. Finicky Friend

Rumor has it Garibaldi invented the accordion,
which he called the Piano of Love. Meanwhile

you're always spilling tobacco when you pull off the filters.
Intimations of the baleful dove:

Prithee, what route did you take to get here,
my fussbudget, my fresh raspberry?

Don't force me to prove in court how I lost it
when I was kidnapped by those academy toughs.

2. Bad Air

The anarchists across the way wear only corduroy
and have taught their pet marmoset to doff his hat and bow—

mocking gesture to a world that's gone flat as a dead pond.
From the bad air the columns are pocked like saltine crackers—

Let them crumble away to dust,
so the past can fill our lungs with cement.

3. The Tower

Once the water supply had been poisoned,
the children got busy knitting mufflers
and swapping morbid stories in the tower.

Soldiers in smart uniforms arrived
with equipment to dredge the canal.
They chatted and smoked and stank up the joint.

One day, like a singing shot of lightning,
your mother will kill you and you won't even know it:

This ham is too salty, you'll think,
or perhaps I need a facial scrub.

4. Palermo

Riding around in this clown car, we can't even see
through the dirty rain pouring down the windshield.
Another tremor in the volcano district. It's unimaginable—

The danger, the cost of electricity, labor. It all adds up.
Like Jane Bowles, we need to change hotels. Ah, if only
you had walked away, what distance there could be between us now.

5. Breaking Training

This summer the box turtle will sing for the first time
in living memory. It was announced in the paper.
Friendly though finicky, you are still reading *Rasselas*
while trying on a priest's collar of many colors.
In the hotel bar, the juncos brood and loll. A lone crusty
grey whale, who came all this way from the Antilles,
asks me if I'll have another. The romp is official.

6. Canaletto

The sky has freed the morning, torn the shreds of fog
away from the bridge with its little wind,

and on the chipped-gilt balcony we make new clouds,
smoking over coffee and chocolate. In your eyes

I see tenderness at war with the comedy of a man's life:
prisoner of your body, and unable to love for long.

7. Rome

How richly this Christ laughed, from deep in the shadows,
as his spirit leapt forth and his body rolled to the stone flags.

Clouds lacerate the sky above the dome. Think
of a vexed train, going round in circles until the end of the world.

These late visions unite as one in my eye;
I finger the thorns and cut myself a slice of suffering.

8. Whistling Past the Grave

The lonely guard yawns, opening wide like a fish.
He comes from the Apennine hills, a massive walled town, and
drives a big black cop car—he claims it's the best in the world.

And I? The pain that laid me flat went prickly
as pizzicati, or—just like water, when it beads on the skin of a grape
then breathes it, eventually, into wine.

These Men with Their Beautiful Eyes

Also flowerpots with their perfect abrasions,
in two colors, foggy cerulean and tarnished canary—

Leg up, the cat washes himself, curled
like a lutist of the Song dynasty—

The days, freighted with gorgeousness,
roll to a full stop.

Voluptuous fruit in the wire basket, taking
soft bruises from the wire—

Wind knocking the pencil to the floor, the papers
to the corners of the room—

Turn those eyes to me again, beautiful eyes
in which I am looking for—

Samaria

Over the deep gorge a bird
circles. Called
"the attorney buzzard,"
he deliberatively draws
a bridge on the air
from one edge of the rim to the sky.
(We cannot walk on air.)
Sudden I smell mimosa,
incongruous as
the drag of your feet, departing
this world
against your will,
against the sun itself.

Intercessionary

At the chalk-hill crossroads
I found your marker, white,

and stood by it begging a day
while the godly gave their small coins.

Once I thought I saw an angel
but it was only your tatty ghost—

the grave-scrape had torn your finery
and you laughed as usual, not minding.

Please: Be my banker,
when my turn comes; vouch for me.

Wheeling

Impossible to call them dead things   those lights
in the sky. Don't tell me   about time;
             it is all now.

.

My Breton ancestor when still a girl
ran away from the turnips and pig-yards of Saint-Perec,
ran away to Paris but was caught by soldiers on the road
and brought back to their service in the fort at Rennes.
This cut-purse Jeanette, strumpet, clever enough
not to die but you'd hardly call that living, to be
bitch of the barracks—

One fine night, spring of 1342 by the old calendar,
two thieves were hanged and then thrown,
according to the commander's whim,
to crackle and stink on a bonfire. My ancestor was sent
to clean the pit that had served as their dungeon,
told she'd have to stay there
if she didn't clean it right.

With a baby slung on her back
she swept the shit, then paused   to look up

through a hole in the thatch.
She could see the moonless dark
and the star-figures she drew as a child on the sky:
the Bear   and the Rooster   all that blackness
pinned and spinning in stately ronde—

the Cat that chases   the Bird
the King's Crown wheeling   toward the Soup Ladle
the Two Donkeys   and there

the Star of Sainte Ghislaine.

.

The stars!

Lisbon, 1989

The new year lurched
on a clamor of horns
trash cans and firecrackers
rising up from the harbor
over the windowsills
into a hotel room where
civility had just died.
Next day we went for lunch
to a pricey restaurant
filled with leftover Nazis
and I was sick in the ladies' room
where the walls were zebra skins
and the vanity stools mothed-up
leopard. So I left alone

for a walk, drank a cold
espresso in a cold café
and reckoned my losses
in the face of lowering rain.
At a bookstore I opened a book
of poems: a few tender lines
about the emerald sea, memory
bringing a smell of salt and roses—
before the words swam back into
Portuguese, indecipherable.
Querido Pessoa, your voice

was clear as music for those
few moments I could read
all the poems ever written.

When I Was Thirteen, I Saw *Uncle Vanya*

A handful of yellow roses
                                        trailing on the stage;
a woman sitting idle on a swing;
charts of "the district"
                                        spread over the floor
while a man and woman
who should not,
                        should,
                                        should not
kiss   leaned over them;
confusion and weeping;
the harness bells shimmering
                                        as the doctor left;
someone saying what he must not say
                                        and then
everyone agreeing it had never been said;
the strange ways music and knocking
came and went—

I kissed the doctor,
I fired the wild shots,
I strummed the guitar,
I poured the tea and
                        dropped the roses
and drank too much and said

"Excuse me, I am without a necktie."
I said, "Live, for once in your life!"

Above me, what I had always called   "sky"
revealed itself a sham:
I took my shiny new knife   and slashed
through the blue paper,
                        to see instead: The real sky,

the high wind bunching and boiling the clouds, and past them,

the unfathomable, planets orange, blue-and-white, magnificent—

Because when I was thirteen, I saw *Uncle Vanya*.

Trying to Like Spenser

Refusal of wit in favor, here, of a knight

in armour so untarnished it glares white—
and on a white horse whose neck curves back
and back, only to bow in swoop, low as if to graze
the greensward, swings low his noble head
as the queen, not faerie-gauzed today but also metalled
ice-white, arrives astride her own white horse.

So hard to take, these apparitions of magnificence

meeting one another in a dark green wood.
They make their own clearing, as we clutch
at *allegory* and then lose it again, it slips away
as even the trees curtsey, abashed by unfamiliar light,
and willow leaves, elves' eyes, shut to silver
and dip low in their own imperceptible breeze.

Just to confuse you, maze on over

and far enough off: in a stubble field six falcons post
in circle aloft, as a foreign knight, black-plumed
and armoured copper red, lies pooled in the crimson
of life poured out his throat. Disdain *symbol*.
A quest, a duel, a murderous errand gone awry?
Mourn him as the sun signals its noon.

Comes an intrusive personal thought:

this noon casts a light I sudden remember
from home movies in Super 8, at the beach,
when the camera's eye slid from perfect blue horizon,
from tomato red-and-yellow stripes of bathing suits,
the checked blanket, the false and silent merry gawping,
up, to the sun itself, burnt white, burnt out.

Now a mossy problem 'mid linnets' clamour, that

in the cool green wood we cannot hear one word
the knight and his queen speak. We guess, since his cross
of red blazes, they plot holy-wise. Unless—fearful thought—
she is no queen but disguised. The horses nicker parley,
some long-standing joke. How I would rather
confer with beasts, breathe in their sour apple air.

Muttering a seemly oath, *by Mary's nose,* I see

that plot full-veiled is Romance unmasked. Let us
tally measures of heavy loveliness, rods' lengths
tapestries of Persia green and Paris blue tugged
from white flanks, tossed to the grass. He and she,
uncarapaced to whitest linen, curl in dalliance
upon silk-broidered peacocks and swans aswim.

It is in the nature of this ordeal, my own crusade

to tame my infidel taste, to continue knowing
that the story of virtue cannot proceed without
the flaring-forth of those gaudy charms and rhymes
that I am since childhood too proud to wear. I choose
dissection and deflection; deeper still lies something
about trust and the wondering largely thereon.

Yet while thus color-stunned; we forgot to ask

where now?—for knight and queen are gone. What
task will queen—glorious one, brittle martial one,
fiend of duplicity, or glitter-cluttered she-bird,
I cannot sort the ladies out and never could—
or knight of tiresome goodness next undertake
with lance or mirror, gilt-hilt dagger or carven cup?

As slight pain swivets my skull, I frantic turn pages

to peasants dancing, delving, and complaining
about the month of March. Join me now: Slap through
those sweetmeat sonnets that stick to your molars,
uxorious bragalamia; and misty notes in which
the poet praises himself. Yet flee though we try, stupored
we are reeled back in to that epic that has no end.

We escape our *Faerie* never; mayhap the last leaves

were burnt up in a fire; the story only pauses. Here
they come again, or else their doubles: knight scaling a cliff
to scold Rue, queen sneering at the moon in stanzas
right casually metered. Elsewhere a maiden (fair)
in kirtle (green) plucks and sings. I hear the lute now,
its ravishing tune I can almost bring myself to hum:

claw-shape the chord: again *strum*, and ever and anon.

Then It Changed

When?
Not sure; I can say
how, but not exactly.
How?
Never sure; I can say
why, extensively.
Why?
Read the poems.
Which ones?
Mine; and better:
    "Then
the tree, at night, began
to change," etcetera.
That explains nothing.
Yes; no. It's not that
I would cease, if I could,
all this brawl and jag,
not at all. More that
a sluice of sweet delight
runs through them now,
because, as said above,
it changed.
When?
Then; now.

notes and acknowledgments

"Not from the Italian" is not from the Italian of 20th-century Milanese poet Viatrix dell'Ombre.

The crying-jags—"The Hyrtl Skulls," "Blossom," "Comet," "If the yellow moon," "Intercessionary," "September," "Jacksonville, Vermont," and "Samaria"—are dedicated to the dead.

In "Then It Changed": "Then the tree, at night, began to change" is from "On the Road Home," by Wallace Stevens.

I am grateful to the editors of the journals where versions of many of these poems first appeared: *American Poet* ("The Hyrtl Skulls"), *Bennington Review* ("Across the Lawn"), *EcoTheo Review* ("Intercessionary"), *Epiphany* ("Not from the Italian"), *Little Star* ("Found Sonnet; Samuel Johnson," "Werner Herzog in the Amazon," "Samaria," "When I was Thirteen, I Saw *Uncle Vanya*," "Trying to Like Spenser"), *The New Republic* ("Wheeling"), *The New York Review of Books* ("Lisbon, 1989"), *Poem-A-Day* ("'Tis Late"), *Poetry* ("Anger," "Bloody Mary"), *Plume* ("Else," "Liliya in Omchak," "Paean for the Players"), *Quarterly West* ("These Men with Their Beautiful Eyes"), *Salmagundi* ("Carnival," "Comet," "City-Born," "Blossom," "Thunder Mountain-Mesa-Valley-Ridge," "Lids"). "Trying to Like Spenser" appeared in the volume *Spenser in the Moment*, edited by Paul J. Hecht and J. B. Lethbridge (Rowman & Littlefield, 2015).

These poems were helped by the generous attentions of Mark Wunderlich, Alice Mattison, Annabel Davis-Goff, Henry Robinson, and Richard Q. Ford.
To them: my thanks and love.